MA...
QUEEN o...

by
ERIC MELVIN

illustrated by
AILEEN PATERSON

ISBN: 1502569353
ISBN-13: 978-1502569356

DEDICATION

This book is dedicated to my dear wife Lynda Melvin whose help and encouragement have always been there.

CONTENTS

ACKNOWLEDGMENTS

This book was originally published by Whigmaleerie Publishing in February 1987 to commemorate the 400th anniversary of the death of Mary, Queen of Scots.

The text of this new edition has been extensively revised and new material added.

I am again grateful to Aileen Paterson, best-known for her 'Maisie' stories about the little kitten which have enchanted children for over 30 years, for permission to use her beautiful illustrations.

Additional background historical information on Mary, Queen of Scots can be freely downloaded at

www.dabsterproductions.com

The candlelight flickered in the draught throwing dancing shadows against the bare stone walls of the cell. Outside an owl hooted as it went in search of its prey. The sentries manning the battlements wrapped themselves deeper into their cloaks and cursed the cold. Their breath hung in clouds around them. The clock in the tower chimed 8 o'clock. Fotheringhay Castle settled itself for the night. The 7th of February 1587 was a night that was not to be forgotten.

Inside the cell a group of people knelt on the floor in silent prayer. There were four of them, three women and a man. They did not look up as the stillness was suddenly broken by the rasping of the lock. The heavy wooden door was swung open, its old iron hinges creaking in protest. The gaoler withdrew his key and stood back. Two armed guards ducked through the low entrance and took up position on either side of the door. The flames from their spluttering torches glowed dully against the darkness of their armour. They each held a drawn sword in their hands. The guards were followed into the cell by a tall, thin man with a long nose and a pointed beard. He wore a richly decorated doublet beneath his heavy, fur-lined cloak.

Behind him came another, older plumper man with a high lace collar and a jewelled hat. The first man stepped forward. In his left hand he carried a decorated staff of office. In his right he carried a rolled up paper. He frowned in distaste when he saw the figures kneeling in prayer

"Madam," he said, "I crave your attention." Still there was no response from the kneeling figures. His face clouded with anger. He was about to stamp his staff and to raise his voice when one of the women crossed herself and made to get up off her knees. She winced as the sharp pain of rheumatism shot through her. The two servant women hurriedly crossed themselves and helped their mistress to her feet. Mary Stuart, Queen of Scots turned to face the man who had interrupted her prayers.

She was a tall woman, forty-five years old and even after nineteen years of imprisonment, it was impossible not to be struck by her beauty. Mary had a long, pointed face with keen, dark, almond eyes. Her reddish-brown hair was partially covered by a white, frilly laced cap. She wore a long black dress with neatly stitched white lace cuffs. A beautiful beaded rosary hung from her neck. Mary reached for this cross and held it tightly in her hand drawing strength and comfort from its touch for the ordeal that she knew lay ahead of her.

Mary nodded a greeting to her visitor, the Earl of Shrewsbury.

"My Lord Shrewsbury," she said, "your visit at this hour is not entirely unexpected, nor, I suspect is the news that you bring me. Come...sit near me where I can hear you. You had better read that paper before it is crushed in your hand."

Lord Shrewsbury squirmed awkwardly before the tall, erect woman. He knew Mary well, having had her in his custody for several of these long years of captivity.

3

Despite his dislike for her Roman Catholic religion, Shrewsbury had always felt some sympathy for the captive Queen.

"Madam," he replied, "I would have greatly desired that another than I should announce to you such sad news as that which I bring you this night. I am commanded by her gracious majesty Queen Elizabeth of England to tell you to prepare yourself for the sentence of death pronounced against you."

There was a gasp from Mary's servants. One of them started to weep. Mary silenced her with a wave of her hand.

"Save your tears Jane Kennedy. It comes as no surprise. I have prepared myself for this for years. Tell me Shrewsbury, am I to be murdered here in my cell?" Shrewsbury shook his head.

"Well then am I to know the hour and manner of my execution, or is to be denied me, as your royal mistress, my dear cousin Elizabeth has denied so much else these long, sorry years?" Mary's eyes flashed with anger.

"No Madam," said Shrewsbury, "I will not deny what you ask. You are to be beheaded tomorrow morning. The sentence is to be carried out at eight o'clock."

Mary closed her eyes and swayed slightly on her feet. Her secretary Sir Andrew Melville moved quickly to her side.

"No, no Sir Andrew," she said, quickly regaining control of herself. "I am all right. It has passed." Mary looked again at the Earl of Shrewsbury who stood shamefaced, his head bowed.

"So my lord, it has come to this. The Queen of Scots is to die the death of a common criminal - and at dawn too. I presume my royal cousin will not be here to witness the show?"

Shrewsbury shook his head. "No, Madam. Her Majesty will not be here."

Mary laughed softly. "And why should she? Elizabeth has refused to see me all these years. She has ignored all my letters, all my appeals for her to visit me here in my wretched cell. I came here as her guest! I threw myself on her mercy after I was unjustly forced to give up my throne. And what mercy has she shown me? Would that our roles had been changed! I would never have allowed my cousin to endure all that I have suffered these nineteen years past! I do not blame you my Lord Shrewsbury. Doubtless you own life could have been at risk if you had shown me too much kindness."

Mary stood for a moment breathing heavily, then composed herself. "But come, these things are not for sharing. I have no doubt that the Earl of Kent skulking there in the shadows behind you is charged to report every word to his royal mistress. Well I will not have it said that Mary Stuart begged for mercy or wept like a child. I thank you my Lord Shrewsbury for the courtesy that you have shown me. I would ask that you now leave me and my servants in peace so that I can prepare myself for tomorrow."

Lord Shrewsbury bowed to Mary and ushered the others out. The heavy door clanged shut behind them. Mary turned to her loyal servants standing around her in shocked silence. She reached for their hands.

"Now my friends, you have served me well for many years. My death will be your release. Please go now to your beds. I want to be left this night to collect my thoughts and prepare myself for God."

Tearfully the three servants obeyed their royal mistress. Mary was left on her own. She went to her seat by the fire and sat down. She reached for her little Highland terrier asleep by the hearth and lifted him up gently. The dog stirred in his sleep, then settled more comfortably on Mary's lap.

Mary leant back in the chair and watched the shadows from the flickering fire dance on the painted ceiling above her head. She let out a deep sigh and felt her body relax. A great weight had been lifted from her. After being under the threat of death for so many years, the news of her execution next morning had come as a blessed relief.

She had been cruelly tricked by Elizabeth's cunning spymaster, Francis Walsingham. If only she had known that her letters were being read and that he had broken her secret code! Instead she had allowed herself to fall into his trap.

She had written to a young English Catholic, Sir Anthony Babington who was part of a plot to replace Queen Elizabeth with the captive Mary. Walsingham had spun a web for Mary and she had been trapped. Her coded letters produced at her trial had sealed her fate. She had been denied any chance to defend herself and had been found guilty. Babington and his fellow plotters had been cruelly executed as traitors.

All hopes and dreams of escape had long since been given up. The thought of being locked up until Death claimed her in withered old age had filled her increasingly with black despair. Now at least she was to be spared that dreadful fate.

Mary sat back and closed her eyes. She gave thanks to God for his mercy. As she approached the last few hours of her life, memories came flooding back to her.

Mary was only six days old when her father King James V of Scotland had died. Mary's uncle Henry VIII, King of England, wanted the child Queen to marry his infant son Edward. Prince of Wales but Mary's mother, Mary of Guise, would have none of it. Twice in 1544 and again in 1547, Henry's armies invaded over the border trying to force his will on poor Scotland.   The destruction of the 'Rough Wooing' was terrible. The great border abbeys of Melrose, Kelso, Dryburgh and Jedburgh were destroyed; Edinburgh was burnt to the ground.

Despite the devastation, the Scots refused to hand over their little Queen to the English. In despair Mary of Guise sent her little daughter for her safety to her family in France. The young child could scarcely have known what was happening to her as she kissed her mother goodbye. It all must have seemed to be a great adventure to the pretty six-year-old. Little did she know that she would only see her mother once more, and then only briefly, when she paid a fleeting visit to France.

Mary sailed for France with four chosen companions – Mary Beaton, Mary Fleming, Mary Livingstone and Mary Seton. These, her *'Four Maries'*, were to remain her closest friends long after childhood. One of them, Mary Seton, shared many of the years of captivity with her beloved royal mistress.

Mary was greeted with all the honour and respect due to a royal visitor. Her radiant beauty charmed the French court. There was though work to be done. She was educated into the duties of a Queen. She learnt several languages; she enjoyed music and showed real talent at sewing beautiful designs onto cloth. Mary delighted in hunting and enjoyed many hours in the saddle.

Mary played happily with the children of the court. She never dreamt for a moment that amidst all that happiness there were those plotting over what should happen to her.

Imagine her surprise to be told that she was to marry Francis, the heir to the French throne. She was still only fifteen years old, while he was a poor sickly youth of fourteen. Mary though had no choice. It was the command of Henry II, King of France.

In 1558 the young couple were wed. All Paris thrilled to the occasion of a royal wedding. Huge crowds lined the decorated streets that led to the great cathedral of Notre Dame. Mary smiled in the glittering wedding coach. The bells rang, the crowds cheered and saluted the young newly-weds.

Mary smiled as the noise of the crowds faded from her memory. "Yes, they were so happy and proud. The bells then were ringing in celebration, not reminding me of my fate on the execution block in the morning. I suppose I was happy in a way. Those were golden days in France. I lacked for nothing. I should have been pleased now that I was married to the heir to of the French throne but I felt that some of my freedom, my precious freedom had gone forever. Francis was so frail and weak that at times I feared for his life. Oh, how quickly can your fortunes change."

Within two years of her marriage, Mary's happiness was shattered by a series of tragedies which began with the loss of her father-in-law, Henry II, mortally wounded in a jousting accident. She was still in mourning when she heard of her mother's death. Mary of Guise had died in Edinburgh Castle in June 1560.

Mary was now Queen of France as well as Queen of Scots. Her husband Francis was the French King. But poor Francis had never been in good health. He never got over the shock of his father's death. He died on 5th December 1560.

Mary's eyes filled with tears as she thought of her husband's funeral.

"Poor, poor Francis. I may not have loved you but I missed you as a friend. I was no longer Queen of France. And I was a widow at nineteen, young and headstrong. I would to God there had been someone that I could have turned to.

Foolishly I chose to return to Scotland, a land that I had not seen for thirteen years. But it was my duty! As I stepped on to the boat I knew then that I would never see dear France again. Oh how right I was!"

A thick mist hung over the port of Leith when Mary arrived on 19th August 1561. The heavy, cold dampness matched her mood. She felt miserable. Even her faithful Maries could not cheer her up.

Everything looked so dull, grey and ugly compared to the France that she had left. What made Mary feel worse was that there was no-one there to welcome her. Her return had taken Edinburgh by surprise. She had to spend her first night back in Scotland in a little house by the harbour. Her Scottish lords came galloping down from Edinburgh next morning.

They greeted her well enough but Mary was struck by the coldness in their eyes. Even her own half-brother, Lord James Stewart, could not hide his displeasure at her arrival. Since her mother's death the previous year, these lords had run Scotland to suit themselves. Now they had a Queen to contend with.

Poor Mary! There was not even a decent horse for her to ride. She had to enter her capital of Edinburgh on an old pony. Her face burned with shame. Crowds had gathered to see the young Queen of Scots. They cheered her on her way but in a half-hearted fashion. Mary could not hide her disappointment with this welcome. She had another shock when she arrived at her Palace of Holyrood. Nothing had been done to prepare it for her. Many of the rooms were cluttered up with workmen's rubbish. How different from the palaces Mary had left behind in France. That night she cried herself to sleep.

The Palace of Holyrood House

Mary soon found out why so many people were cold towards her. As a good Catholic she had arranged to hear Mass as usual with her priest the next morning. Word must somehow have got out and a raging mob tried to storm the Palace. Lord James and his guards only just managed to hold them back. Shaken, Mary confronted her half-brother.

"My Lord James, in God's name what does this mean?" she demanded. The tall, handsome bearded man looked haughtily down on her. "It seems my dear sister, that you have forgotten something." he said.

Mary frowned. "I am sorry but I do not understand your meaning. I attend Mass as I usually do and find myself threatened by a noisy mob. Pray explain to me what it is that I have forgotten."

"Madam," he replied, "you have forgotten that Scotland is now a Protestant country following the teachings of the true Reformed Church. The Pope in Rome has no longer any power left in this country.

You had better appreciate that Parliament has ended his authority and all the superstitious nonsense that styles itself the Catholic religion."

Mary gasped in horror, "I had heard talk of such foolishness while I was in France but I could not believe that my people would risk the wrath of God and put their eternal souls in danger. Surely the Pope holds the keys to the Kingdom of Heaven?"

James laughed mockingly. "The keys to Hell more like! I warn you sister that if you make a public show of your papist ways then I cannot be answerable for your safety." With that he gave a curt bow, turned on his heel and left Mary shaking her head in bewilderment.

The sudden screeching of an owl startled the captive Queen. She reached for her cucifix and held it tight.

"Why , oh why can people not be allowed to worship God freely? That was what I wanted for my country but they would have me outlaw the Catholic religion and abandon my faith. My God, what I had to endure from their madness and threats. Worst of all was that rabble-rouser John Knox. To have heard him shout at me, you could never have believed that I was his Queen. I wonder what would have happened if I had locked him up in my deepest dungeon?"

Despite the religious problems, Mary managed to govern Scotland well for four years, travelling far and wide throughout the country to meet her people and to administer justice in her royal courts. Her travels took her to such great castles as Doune, near Stirling, Dunottar near Aberdeen, Blair near Blair Atholl and Spynie near Nairn.

Dunottar Castle

Mary became particularly fond of Falkland Palace in Fife which her father James V had rebuilt in French style for his Queen, Mary of Guise. This magnificent palace must have reminded Mary of those grand palaces she had known in France.

Falkland Palace

Alone in the flickering stillness of Fotheringhay, Mary struggled to hold on to the reassuring images of sunlight and laughter. But it was no use. Always the nightmares returned.

"How I wish I had had the good sense not to marry again! At least I can agree with my cousin Queen Elizabeth about that. She has never married and seems determined not to take a husband. Would that I had resolved to do the same! My marriages have only brought me pain and unhappiness."

But as a beautiful young widow, Mary found herself under pressure to marry again. Her Scots' lords were forever urging her to find another husband. Scotland needed an heir to the throne. All sorts of princes and nobles were suggested as suitable husbands for her but Mary soon became impatient with this interference in her life.

It was at a ball at Holyrood in 1565 that Mary first saw her cousin Henry, Lord Darnley. She was captivated by the good looks of the tall, handsome young man. He too found her very attractive. Henry was also very ambitious. Marriage to the Queen of Scots would make him the most powerful man in the land. Mary gave no thought to this. Instead she found herself falling hopelessly in love with Danley.

Some of her lords tried to prevent them seeing each other. Lord James warned her that such a marriage would turn many of her supporters against her. Mary paid no heed to these warnings. She was in love.

So she and Darnley were married later that year in a quiet service at Holyrood Palace. How different from her wedding to Francis at Notre Dame! It was not long however before Mary realised that there was a darker side to her husband's character. As well as being ambitious, he was a vain, cruel man. He drank heavily and had a vicious temper. Darnley could behave like a spoilt child if he did not get his way. Despite his pleas, Mary refused to have Darnley crowned as King. This just added to his frequent bursts of bad temper.

Mary came to hate and despise her husband. Yet who could she turn to for help and support? She did not trust Lord James, a man also ambitious for power. Most of her other lords had not forgiven her for marrying Darnley against their advice

Unlike her cousin Queen Elizabeth who was guided by a small group of loyal advisers, Mary was dangerously isolated. More and more, she found comfort and friendship with a close group of beloved servants, particularly her *'Four Maries'* and her handsome Italian secretary, David Rizzio.

On the night of 9th March 1566 a small supper party was held in Mary's private chamber at Holyrood Palace. It had been a long, hard winter. Mary was expecting a baby and had not been well. So a group of her friends had arranged this party to help to cheer their royal mistress up.

The evening had been a great success. There had been laughter and joking. David Rizzio sat by the fire playing his guitar and singing in his beautiful voice. Mary's eyes sparkled in the candlelight. She felt better than she had felt for months. Then without warning the door swung open. There stood Darnley. He was horribly drunk. He said nothing but stumbled across the room to an empty chair. He flung himself down.

Darnley sat with a scowl on his face and demanded some wine. He drained his cup and then sat back as though expecting something to happen. Mary was puzzled but decided to leave Darnley to drink himself to sleep. It would not be the first time that this had happened. Suddenly there was the sound of rushing footsteps pounding up the stairs. The door was flung open and a group of armed men rushed in with weapons drawn. Theere were cries of terror as Mary's guests shrank back in fear. She though sprang to her feet and bravely stood her ground.

"In God's name what on earth do you mean by bursting into my chambers like this?" she cried.

Their leader stepped forward and raised the visor of his helmet. In the torchlight Mary could see the pale, sickly face of Lord Ruthven, one of her husband's close friends. He roughly pushed Mary to one side and sat down on a chair. He rudely put his feet up on the table and called for a cup of wine. Mary's eyes blazed with fury.

"My Lord Ruthven!" she shouted. "Explain this infamous conduct on your part or you will answer for it with your life!"

Lord Ruthven put down his cup and wiped his mouth with the back of his hand. "My infamous conduct? Why no, your Majesty, we have come to rescue you from the infamous conduct of another."

He laughed out loud. His men joined in the cruel, mocking laughter. Lord Ruthven continued.

"You must know your Majesty, that we, your loyal subjects, are much distressed at the way this wretched Italian has abused you."

Lord Ruthven pointed his mailed finger towards David Rizzio.

Mary gasped in horror. "No! No!" she cried. "You are mistaken. This man is my loyal servant. He has never wronged me. If any of you have any doubt then let him bring a charge to Parliament. Now go before my guards come to arrest you as traitors!"

"Enough!" roared Lord Ruthven. "Seize him!"

David Rizzio cried out and ran behind Mary. He clutched hold of her skirts begging for mercy. It was no use. Fierce hands dragged him away. Mary tried to protect him but she was roughly grabbed by one of the men who held a dagger to her throat. She could only watch in horror as David Rizzio was butchered in front of her. She shut her eyes as knives rose and fell into his body. Then it was all over. The men left, slamming the door behind them. David Rizzio lay in a pool of blood on the floor.

At the sound of the tower bell, Mary started. *"Is that another hour past so soon? And still so much to remember. At least there will be no more nightmares thank God.   How many times have I woken up sweating with David's pitiful cries for help ringing in my ears? Yes and how often have I seen my husband sitting in his chair watching the horrid spectacle? Worthless coward that he was! He planned it all but left it to others to carry out that foul murder. If only the fool had known that he had signed his own death warrant by his infamous conduct   against me and my friends.. Foolish Henry Darnley!"*

In the summer of 1566 Mary had given birth to a son James in Edinburgh Castle. She had hoped perhaps that having a son might change Darnley for the better. But it was not to be. Darnley showed little interest in James and behaved as badly as ever.

Mary was deeply hurt by his shameful conduct. She now longed to be rid of him. She decided to try to divorce Darnley but who could she turn to for advice? Then Francis Hepburn, the powerful Earl of Bothwell came into her life. To Mary, a lonely, much-wronged woman,   it seemed that God had answered her prayers. Bothwell seemed to be everything that her husband was not. He was decisive, bold, courageous and strong. His dark, brooding eyes captivated Mary, She had been sent a champion.

Francis Hepburn, the Earl of Bothwell

Mary poured out her troubled heart to him. She told him all about Darnley's wickedness and how she longed to be free. In her excitement, Mary threw caution to the winds. While staying in Jedburgh in October 1566 she heard that Bothwell had been badly wounded in a fight with outlaws and lay perhaps at death's door in Hermitage Castle some 50 kms away. Mary rode through the night to be by his side. This was a serious error of judgement. She should have known that her action would start people talking about her friendship with Bothwell, but Mary's servants were too frightened to warn her of the terrible rumours that were now being spread.

Then Darnley fell ill. Word came that he had been struck down by the dreadful smallpox while on a visit to one of his parents in Glasgow. Mary now took pity on her pathetic husband and resolved to nurse him herself. By this concern she hoped that the horrid talk about her and Bothwell might stop.

Mary had Darnley brought back to Edinburgh. He was lodged in a house at Kirk o' Field just outside the burgh walls and not far from Holyrood Palace. Each day Mary went to visit him but she found it hard not to be repelled by the sight of his once-handsome face dreadfully scarred by the smallpox.

There was though something for Mary to look forward to that February 1567. One of her favourite servants was to be married at Holyrood. The day of the wedding arrived. Mary visited Darnley as usual then hastened back to change. After the wedding service, a ball was to be held in the Palace.

It was a wonderful evening. Amongst the glittering company, Mary seemed to dance away her cares.

Few noticed that Bothwell excused himself and left the ballroom. He was gone for some time. The ball was nearly over before he re-appeared.

Suddenly the whole palace was shaken by a tremendous explosion. People screamed in terror as the force of the blast rattled the window shutters. Bothwell and some of the others drew their swords and ran off into the night to discover what was wrong. Mary sat waiting, overwhelmed by an awful feeling of dread.

It was Bothwell himself who returned to tell Mary that the house at Kirk o' Field had been blown up. But there was no sign of Darnley in the wreckage. It was only later that the searchers had found him. Darnley and one of his servants were there lying dead in a nearby garden. Darnley had been murdered. Mary's husband was dead.

There seemed to be only one man whom Mary could turn to in her anguish – Bothwell. He alone seemed prepared to defend her from her enemies. Mary appealed to Bothwell for help. The help that she got though was far more than she bargained for.

Mary was returning to Edinburgh that April having visited her son James in Stirling. As she crossed the River Almond at Linlithgow, Bothwell, accompanied by a large troop of armed horsemen, rode up to meet her. Before Mary could do or say anything, Bothwell seized the reins of her horse and galloped her away to his castle at Dunbar.

Mary was at his mercy. She now acted with a foolishness born out of desperation. She granted Bothwell a divorce from his wife and only three months after Darnley's murder, agreed to wed him. Marrying the man many people believed to be one of the murderers of Darnley was an act of folly that turned her people against her.

A group of her most powerful lords raised an army to oppose her. Mary and Bothwell gathered what few supporters they could. At Carberry, outside Musselburgh, Mary and Bothwell confronted the forces that were drawn up against them.

Commanding that army was her own half-brother, Lord James Stuart, now the Earl of Moray. The position was hopeless. Bothwell abandoned Mary to the mercy of their enemies and fled for his life. They would never meet again. Rather than risk bloodshed, Mary surrendered and was led from the field in tears.

A tear trickled down Mary's cheek. She brushed it away. *"Oh God, how blind I was to have trusted Bothwell. He was no better than the rest. In fact he was worse. A cruel wicked fiend who deceived me terribly. God knows how he abused me and yet at the same time I saw him as a a man of strength; a man ready to defend his Queen from her foes; a man worthy of my love.*

I know what was said then and I know what is still said today. That Mary Stuart plotted with her lover to murder Henry Darnley. Why they even produced letters to prove it. Worthless forgeries, that is all they are! I could have shown that easily but they never had the courage to let me see them at my trial. Well as God is my witness I did not kill my husband. Whatever wrong I have done in my life – and I have done wrong – then God will surely judge me".

Mary was taken to Edinburgh and spent a last night in her capital in the Provost's house in the High Street. She could not sleep for the noise of an angry crowd baying at her window. From Edinburgh, Mary was sent as a prisoner to gloomy Loch Leven Castle.

By this time she was tired, depressed and ill. She must have felt that she was going to her certain death as she was rowed across the loch. Mary trembled with fear as she was hustled roughly through the castle entrance. Mary was conscious of the curious stares of the soldiers on the castle walls. A small crowd had gathered in the courtyard to watch the broken Queen.

The heavy wooden door clanged shut behind her. She looked round the hard faces of the guards. There was no pity to be seen in their eyes. She breathed a silent prayer and prepared herself for death.

Loch Leven Castle

Sir William Douglas, the keeper of Loch Leven Castle, stepped forward and looked with contempt at the pathetic figure of Mary. "Madam", he said. "I am commanded by the Earl of Moray and the other Lords in Council to hold you here as my prisoner until such time as they shall decide what is to become of you. There is no point in wasting your energies with thoughts of escape. No-one has ever escaped from this castle. Instead I would suggest that you spend your time asking God's forgiveness for your wickedness!".

Mary's cheeks burned with shame. Tearfully she was led to the room set aside for the royal prisoner. As the door closed behind her she must have thought her position to be hopeless.

For days Mary was in black despair. She refused to eat or drink. Soon she was too weak to move from her bed. She suffered terribly. Then her half-brother, James, the Earl of Moray, came to see her. He could not hide the disgust from his face when he saw Mary in her misery. She looked up at him with a tear-stained face.

"So brother are you here to murder me? You have always been greedy for power in this kingdom."

"No." he growled. "You are not going to be killed just yet. Your life though hangs by a thread. Unless you agree to give up the throne in favour of your son you have but a short time to live."

Mary gasped with shock. "Abdicate? You mean me to give up my crown? But James is only a little child. He cannot be expected to rule Scotland."

The Earl of Moray laughed wickedly. "No of course he cannot. But I can and by this piece of paper I will. When you agree to give up the throne I will act as Regent for my dear little nephew until he is old enough to rule for himself."

Mary's eyes filled with tears. There seemed to be no choice. What could she do but sign away her crown?.

"How quiet it is. As quiet as it was that night in my room at Loch Leven. I had lost my throne and my son. I never saw him again. By my own foolishness I had lost everything. I had been blind to the greedy ambition of those who should have been loyal to me. Now they had triumphed. I was at their mercy.

There seemed little purpose in life after that. For weeks I just lay on my bed not caring if I lived or died. But I found that I still had friends loyal to me. George Douglas, brother of my gaoler, was a dashing young man then. While his cousin, Willie Douglas was but a lad in his teens."

These two young men were determined to help Mary escape. The first plan devised by George failed and he was banished from the island. But in the spring of 1568 young Willie came forward with a desperate plan of his own.

In the castle out of earshot of any of the guards he outlined his bold idea to Mary. "Your Grace, I have received word from George. Lord Seton and some of your friends are waiting for you across the water in Kinross."

"But Willie," replied Mary. "how on earth can I reach them? I am so closely watched now. I am not even permitted to walk near the lochside let alone have you row me in your boat as you used to do."

"Your Grace, tomorrow is May Day. Now, there is a custom here on the island to celebrate the start of summer by dressing up and enjoying ourselves." "Yes," said Mary, "I have heard the servants talk about it. But how can this help me to escape?"

"Your Grace," explained Willie, "I have been chosen to be the Abbot of Unreason tomorrow." "The Abbot of Unreason?" asked Mary. "What nonsense is this?"

"The Abbot of Unreason," explained Willie, "is in charge of the celebrations. People must dress up in fancy costumes and follow me in the dance. They must do whatever I do." Willie smiled. "I promise you your Grace, that by tomorrow evening they will all be so tired and so drunk that they will not notice us slipping away. You must dress up and take part as well. They will not mind you doing that. But in the afternoon you must excuse yourself.

"What then?" asked Mary?

"Pretend that you have a headache. Go back to your room and dress yourself as a servant. I will come for you when it is time to go."

Mary was astonished at what Willie was suggesting. Perhaps indeed there was a chance. She frowned. "But what about the keys Willie? The castle gate will be locked against us."

Willie nodded his head. "Aye there is a problem there. Sir William keeps the keys on his belt at all times. There is one chance though. I have noticed when I serve him at table that he puts the keys down beside him. Somehow I will try to take them from the table without him noticing. But come now, we must part your Grace lest the guards get suspicious. Play your part tomorrow as I have told you and be ready for me by suppertime. With God's help we will succeed."

And succeed they did! May Day was a hot sunny day. Willie danced his way around the castle and the castle grounds. By evening everyone was exhausted. At supper, Willie covered the keys with a napkin and took them. Sir William was too drunk to notice.

 Willie collected Mary from her room. Together they made their way quickly to Willie's rowing boat moored by the lochside. Behind them they could hear the sounds of singing and merrymaking.

Willie rowed Mary over the loch to a spot where George and some friends were waiting with horses. Together they galloped off towards Lord Seton's castle at Niddrie. Mary breathed in the cool air of the evening and laughed out loud. She was free!

"Is that another hour gone already? Surely not. Why is it that I have had to suffer the passing of the hours dragging at a snail's pace all these long years of captivity when now, when my time has almost come, the hours seem to be flashing by. And yet my memories are all but over.

Perhaps it is just as well. Like the hours this night my freedom after my escape did not last for long. I had no time to raise an army. My enemies were close behind. I gathered my few followers at Hamilton but they were scattered at Langside and I was forced to flee once more. Oh, how I wish that I had gone back to France! That was what my friends urged me to do. Instead I chose to go to England to seek shelter from my cousin Queen Elizabeth."

On her arrival in England, Mary was taken to Carlisle Castle where the surprised governor considered what was to be done with this royal refugee. Word was quickly sent to London. While Elizabeth and her advisers debated Mary's future, she was moved to Bolton Castle.

In the meantime, Elizabeth ordered an inquiry to be held at York to investigate the accusations that had been made against Mary. However the inquiry was inconclusive and so began Mary's journey from one English residence to another – Turbury Castle, Wingfield Manor, Chatsworth Manor and Sheffield.

The problem for Mary was that for English Catholics she was seen as the rightful Queen of England. To them Elizabeth was illegitimate as the Pope had never given permission for her father Henry VIII to divorce his wife to marry Elizabeth's mother, Anne Boleyn. Gradually Mary became aware of many English Catholics who were sympathetic towards her plight. A plot by the Catholic Earl of Norfolk to free Mary failed. Others though were determined to remove Elizabeth and replace her with Mary.

Some fourteen years later Mary was tricked into writing secret letters to English Catholics whom she still hoped might set her free. It was these letters to Sir Anthony Babington which led to her arrest and trial at Fotheringhay Castle in October 1586.

Mary wrung her hands in despair.

"Nineteen years. Nineteen wasted years..." A tear trickled slowly down her cheek. She shook her head and half-closed her eyes. "I think that I have seen the inside of fourteen different castles in that time. It is so many now that I can scarcely remember their names. And in all that time Elizabeth and I have never seen each other; we have never met face to face despite all my appeals to her even answer my letters, instead she has cruelly condemned me to death.

Believe me Elizabeth, I never wanted your throne. God knows that there are Catholics here in England who would see me as their rightful Queen in your place. But I have never wished ill of you. All that I have ever wanted is my freedom.

I should have known that you would have had my letters opened and read. Perhaps I was careless in what I wrote to Babington but I just wanted to be released from my captivity. As God is my witness I did not seek your murder Elizabeth.

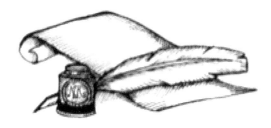

I wonder if my execution will be on your conscience? Merciful heaven, but it should be! There is one thing though that I know will keep you awake at night. You may kill me but you can not kill my son. You, Elizabeth, will end your days childless. You will go to your grave knowing that James, the son of Mary, Queen of Scots, will then sit on your throne. And after that, God willing, his children and his grandchildren will wear the crowns of Scotland and England. Think of that after I am gone. But enough of this. It will soon be dawn. I must seek God's forgiveness for my sins."

Her prayers finished, Mary woke her servants. They dressed her in black. Shortly before 8 o'clock Mary was led from her cell into the great hall of Fotheringhay Castle where a large wooden scaffold had been erected. There in the chill February air a small crowd had gathered to witness her execution.

A grim-faced official read out the sentence of execution against her. Mary was guilty of plotting the death of Queen Elizabeth. Mary stared at him with a glint of defiance in her eyes. Then she was ready.

As she was helped up the steps, a thin shaft of sunlight caught her golden-red hair and lit up her pale face. Mary took a tearful farewell of her devoted servants and knelt to pray.

She rose up and looked at the bearded executioner who stood leaning on his gleaming axe.

"I forgive you for what you have to do this day." said Mary. "You are not to blame for my death."

The executioner bowed towards her. A blindfold was now tied round Mary's eyes. She knelt and placed her head on the block, her crucifix held tightly in her hand. "Into your hands O Lord...."

Then the executioner struck. But he did not strike cleanly. It took two more blows of his axe before Mary's head was cut off. The executioner bent down to pick it up. "So perish all traitors!" he shouted.

There was a horrified gasp from the spectators as Mary's head fell from his hand and he was left holding a wig. The long year's of captivity had left Mary's hair thin and grey. When they came to take her body away thay found her little Highland terrier cowering beneath her skirt unwilling to leave his dead mistress, Mary, Queen of Scots.

Mary was buried at nearby Peterborough Cathedral. In 1612, her son James, who had indeed become King of England on Elizabeth's death in 1603, had his mother's body taken to Westminster Abbey.

Remember that Mary was only six years old when she left for France. She was a widow of nineteen when she returned to Scotland. Mary actually ruled over Scotland for less than seven years before her forced abdication and flight to England. These years were darkened by intrigue and murder. David Rizzio and Henry, Lord Darnley both met violent deaths.

Was Mary a party to these plots or was she swept along helplessly by a tide over which she had little control? We will never know the full story of those years. What we do know is that Mary, Queen of Scots remains the tragic heroine of Scotland.

Mary was very talented at embroidery. While a prisoner in England she embroidered a beautiful cloth and added the words which have become her motto:

"En ma fin git mon Commencement"

Which translates as: *"In my end is my beginning"*.

Fitting last words for Mary.

Places to Visit in Scotland

1. **The Palace of Holyroodhouse.** Mary lived in the Palace for six years. Many dramatic events took place here including the murder of David Rizzio in March 1566.
2. **Edinburgh Castle.** Within the Royal Apartments, Mary gave birth to her son James VI (later James I of the United Kingdom of England and Scotland).
3. **Linlithgow Palace.** Birthplace of Mary.
4. **Loch Leven Castle.** Mary was imprisoned here and forced to abdicate. She escaped in May 1568.
5. **Stirling Castle.** Much of Mary's early childhood was spent here before she was sent to France in 1548.
6. **Blair Castle, Blair Atholl.** One of the many castles that Mary stayed in on her travels round Scotland.
7. **Spynie Palace, near Elgin.** Mary stayed here in 1562.
8. **Traquhair House, near Peebles.** This claims to be the oldest inhabited house in Scotland. Mary was here with Darnley in 1566.
9. **Hermitage Castle near Langholm.** Mary made her famous ride from Jedburgh to visit the wounded Bothwell here in October 1566.

10. **Queen Mary's House, Jedburgh.** This house claims to be house where Mary stayed in October 1566. It is now a museum dedicated to Mary.
11. **Crichton Castle, near Pathhead.** A Bothwell family castle.
12. **Hailes Castle, near East Linton.** Another Bothwell family castle
13. **Dunbar Castle.** Another Bothwell family castle.
14. **Arbroath Abbey.** Visited by Mary in 1562.
15. **Falkland Palace.** Visited by Mary who enjoyed hunting in the surrounding countryside.

For further information on Mary, Queen of Scots in Scotland contact:

VisitScotland,
94 Ocean Drive,
Edinburgh EH6 6JH.

www.visitscotland.com

info@visitscotland.com

Places to Visit in England.

1. **Bolton Castle, Wensleydale.** Mary was imprisoned here between 1568 and 1569.
2. **Wingfield Manor, South Wingfield.** Another prison for Mary.
3. **Turberry Castle, Burton-on-Trent.** Mary was imprisoned here twice.
4. **Fotheringhay Castle, near Oundle.** Only a grassy mound remains to mark the site of the castle where Mary was executed in February 1587.
5. **Peterborough Cathedral.** Mary was buried here after her execution.
6. **Westminster Abbey.** From 1612, the tomb of Mary, Queen of Scots.

For information on Mary, Queen of Scots in England contact:

VisitEngland,
Sanctuary Buildings,
20 Great South Stree,t
London SW1P 3BT.

www.visitengland.com

attractions@visitengland.org

ABOUT THE AUTHOR

Eric Melvin graduated with First Class Honours in History and Political Thought from Edinburgh University in 1967. He qualified as a Secondary teacher of History and Modern Studies. He retired from teaching in 2005, working latterly as Headteacher at Currie Community High School.

In addition to teaching History at school, Eric has for many years taken Community Education classes for The City of Edinburgh in both Scottish History and The History of Edinburgh. He also give talks to various groups on aspects of the City's History. (e.g. Probus and Local History Clubs). Eric is a trained volunteer guide for The Edinburgh Festival Voluntary Guides Association and regularly takes groups down the Royal Mile and through the New Town.

Eric has had several books published for younger readers on aspects of Scottish History. He is the author of 'A Walk Down Edinburgh's Royal Mile' and the companion volume 'A Walk Through Edinburgh's New Town' - both also published in 2014.

Eric is a member of the High Constables of Edinburgh, the historic bodyguard of Edinburgh's Lord Provost who act as an escort on ceremonial occasions. He works voluntarily in the Oxfam Bookshop at Morningside and has done voluntary teaching in Chogoria Girls' High School in Kenya.

Eric is married to Lynda, a retired Nursery School Teacher. They have two sons, John currently lecturing in Heritage Tourism at Hosei University in Tokyo and Graeme, also working in Tokyo as a Business Communications Skills Trainer for American Express. John is married to Shizue Ichikawa from Sakata in Japan. They are the proud parents of Isla, a first grand-child, born in August 2010 and Rui born in April 2013.

31088397R00035

Printed in Great Britain
by Amazon